IMAGES
of England

AROUND ABINGDON
THE SECOND SELECTION

Abingdon School 1st IV, 1896. From left: C.A.W. Payne (bow), B. Challenor (3), A.W. Morland (stroke), L.F. Gale (cox), W.B. Collingwood (2). The school rowing club was one of the first boat clubs on the Thames and documented as active in 1840. L.F. Gale (1885-1915) was killed on the Western Front at Ypres while serving with the Queen's Own Oxfordshire Hussars. A.W. Morland (1878-1942) served in the South African War and First World War from 1916, he was mayor of Abingdon 1913-15 and director of Morland's brewery until his death. Bromley Challenor (1879-1963), the third generation of Abingdon solicitors, admitted 1904, awarded an OBE in 1918, and was Abingdon coroner, clerk to the justices, commissioner of income tax and superintendent registrar.

IMAGES
of England

AROUND
ABINGDON
THE SECOND SELECTION

Nigel Hammond

TEMPUS

Market Place, 1857. An obelisk stood in the market from 1834 until replaced by a statue of Queen Victoria, presented by Mr Edwin Trendell in 1887 for the golden jubilee. The obelisk was then removed to the Square.

First published 2002

Tempus Publishing Limited
The Mill, Brimscombe Port,
Stroud, Gloucestershire, GL5 2QG

British Library Cataloguing in Publication Data.
A catalogue record for this book is available from the British Library.

ISBN 0 7524 2649 4

Typesetting and origination by Tempus Publishing Limited
Printed in Great Britain by Midway Colour Print, Wiltshire

Contents

Introduction   7

1.   Old Abingdon   9

2.   Christ's Hospital   19

3.   School   29

4.   Moving Around   43

5.   The Berkshire Yeomanry 1900-1919   55

6.   Trade and Business   75

7.   People   87

8.   Work and Play   101

9.   Abingdon and the Villages   109

Acknowledgements   128

Bibliography   128

John Rocque's map of Berkshire, 1761. The small size of Abingdon is shown with its relationship to villages in the vicinity of the county town.

6

Introduction

Born to a Puritan and anti-monarchist Wiltshire family, Celia Fiennes (1662-1741), travelled through England between 1685 and 1703 by coach and on horseback, recording vivid descriptions of her journeys, commenting on the towns, roads, inns, local buildings, trade and industry by which she passed. Her entry to Abingdon, then county town of Berkshire, was by way of Culham Bridge, the causeway over Andersey Island, and across the ancient Borough Ford Bridge of 1416. Celia Fiennes wrote in her diaries:

'I went to Abington and cross'd the River Thames on a bridge atte the end of the town, and so entered into Berkshire and rode along by the Thames a good way, which was full of Barges and lighters. Abington town seems a very well built town and the Market Cross is the finest in England.'

Misnaming the decorative market cross, which had been demolished by the Parliamentarians under General Waller during the civil war, for the magnificent market or county hall built by Christopher Kempster, influenced by Sir Christopher Wren and freshly completed in 1677, she observed '…its all freestone and very lofty, even the Isles of Walk below is a lofty arch on severall pillars of square stone and four square pillars, over it are large Roomes with handsome Windows.'

Parts of the scene she portrays will be recognised by present day Abingdonians, having on market-day Monday numerous stalls gathered in the market place and part of the farmers' market under the shelter of the county hall.

The eighteenth and nineteenth centuries were a fascinating and largely prosperous period for Abingdon: the town thrived as county town of Berkshire, as an agricultural market and a centre for medium-scale manufacturing, commerce, and trade. John Roysse's Free School flourished under the headship of the Revd Thomas Woods, (Tesdale Usher then headmaster 1711- 53), offering an education to both the sons of the poor of Abingdon and to the sons of the wealthy and titled in neighbouring county families. The established church at St Helen's had notable incumbents. Joseph Newcome (1719-57), whose son William progressed though the Irish episcopate to become Archbishop of Armagh (1795-1800); John Cleobury (1775-1800), whose three sons also progressed through the grammar school to distinguished academic and clerical careers.

In the nineteenth century notable St Helen's incumbents included: Charles Sumner (1821-22), became Bishop of Winchester (1827-69); Hugh Pearson (1822-23), was Dean of Salisbury (1823-46); John Turner (1823-24), became Bishop of Calcutta. Nathaniel Dodson's long incumbency (1824-67) was marked by a revival of church life in the town, associated with the developing Oxford Movement. Archdeacon Alfred Pott (1868-74), an early protégé of Bishop Wilberforce of Oxford, worked to update the church schools and to reorganise and restore the church fabric. For its last quarter of a century in the town centre, the grammar school was in the capable and dedicated hands of old boy, Dr William Alder Strange (headmaster 1840-68).

By 1869 Abingdon had lost its cherished county town status to the much-expanded Reading. A decline had already set in when the Great Western Railway extension to Oxford in 1844 passed not as originally intended from Steventon to Abingdon thence Oxford, due to opposition from both townspeople and corporation, but from Didcot east of the town through Appleford and Radley. The failure to secure the railway helped to seal Abingdon's slow decline.

The twentieth century dawned with the South African war, this, followed within twenty years by the First World War, in common with much of the country, had a traumatic and devastating effect on Abingdon. Prior to 1914 men from trade and farming communities in both town and neighbouring countryside, often as a matter of course, volunteered and trained, most with the Berkshire Yeomanry, some with The Queen's Own Oxfordshire Hussars. The Yeomanry held annual camps nearby, at Churn on the Berkshire Downs above Blewbury on part of Lord Wantage's Lockinge Estate. Many of those volunteers were to perish at Gallipoli and in Palestine, as were other Abingdonians who joined the Royal Navy, Merchant Navy or the Royal Berkshire Regiment while fighting on the Western front.

The Berkshire Yeomanry had a distinguished and unique history, raised first in 1794 when the Lord Lieutenant was invited to form a non-regular volunteer force of cavalry and infantry to resist any French invasion by Napoleon Bonaparte. The infantry came largely from unskilled workers, the cavalry from the farmers and tradesmen and it was officered by the county gentry. The *Reading Mercury* of 21 April 1794 noted the formation of an Abingdon mounted troop styled the Abingdon Independent Cavalry, commanded by Capt Thomas Prince. But no French invasion came and in 1804 the Abingdon, Hungerford, Donnington with Newbury and Vale of the White Horse troops were formed into the first regiment of the Royal Berkshire Yeomanry Cavalry.

By 1894 Abingdon came under D squadron, the Wantage Troop, which recruited from North Berkshire. They went through the South African war and inevitably into the First World War. Brigaded with the Queen's Own Oxfordshire Hussars and the Royal Bucks Hussars, the Berkshire Yeomanry formed part of the 2nd South Midland Brigade. In April 1915 they were sent to Egypt and in August to the Dardanelles landing at A beach east of Suvla on 18 August 1915. Fighting at the battles of Chocolate Hill (Hill 53) and Scimitar Hill (Hill 70), the Berkshire Yeomanry went into action, three days after landing, with 9 officers and 314 men, returning with 4 officers and 150 men. Casualties were 5 officers and 164 men. The Yeomanry remained in defence for three months then withdrew on 1 November 1915 for Egypt. 'The evacuation from Gallipoli was the only well executed part of a disastrous campaign.' By January 1917, the Berkshire Yeomanry, ordered to the Middle East, advanced from Sinai to Gaza. At the first battle of Gaza (26-27 March 1917) the enemy was well prepared and in foggy conditions the Yeomanry withdrew. In the second battle of Gaza (17-19 April 1917), Major Philip Wroughton who commanded D Squadron was fatally wounded by shellfire and the troops were ordered to retire. There is a granite memorial to Philip Wroughton on Woolley Down above Wantage, where each April wreaths are placed by descendants of the Yeomanry, to 'an outstanding officer much mourned by his regiment' and to the other officers and men who served in this campaign.

Between the wars Abingdon saw major housing expansion at the Workhouse and Boxhill sites off Oxford Road and south in Saxton Road. The MG Car Company took over a leather factory in 1929 and made Abingdon famous worldwide through its competitions department and by sales to the American market. The Royal Air Force Station was built over Abingdon Golf Course in the 1930s. In the last fifty years Abingdon has continued to expand and prosper. Post-war development of the Atomic Energy Research Establishment at Harwell brought further housing together with injection of a new intellectual elite to the town. The MG factory has gone, so has the much lamented Morland Brewery. Disappearing too over time, the manufacture of canal and river barges, clothing, sacking, carpets, malt and leather. The AERE site and RAF station have downsized and transformed, the latter replaced by Dalton Barracks and the Royal Logistics Corps. Light industry and service activity mushrooms on trading estates with new housing and fresh roads on the outer fringes of the town but as yet there are no plans for a new river bridge to relieve traffic congestion over the bridge of 1416 and in the town centre.

Although Celia Fiennes would find much of today's Abingdon unrecognisable, except perhaps for the immediate town centre, I suspect she would still be able to comment in a positive spirit, on the 'roads, inns, local buildings, trade and industry' she would see.

Nigel Hammond
August 2002

One
Old Abingdon

The Gaol, c. 1855. Abingdon gaol opened in 1811 retaining the Assizes and county town status. The gaol closed in 1868, and the Assize court and county town status were lost to Reading in 1869. The Waterman inn (right) had river and street entrances. The boat was to ferry patrons to and from premises and wharves along the river. In 1853 the service was provided by George Davis, victualler.

County Hall, *c.* 1805. Print engraved by R. Roffe from a drawing by G. Shepherd. From the roof Abingdon's unique bun-throwing ceremony takes place. Cakes and buns were distributed on royal occasions; the coronation of George IV in 1821 saw a thousand penny cakes disposed of and for the coronation of William IV in 1831 five hundred penny cakes went. The first reference to 'throwing' was at the coronation of Victoria, but was 'according to custom', which implies earlier origin.

The Half Moon, East St Helen Street, *c.* 1855. The landlord was William Horner, beer retailer. The inn stood near the coaling wharves and small manufacturing workshops in the area from which it partly took its clientele. The inn closed around 1922.

Market Place, *c.* 1855. From the left, St Nicolas' church, grammar school entrance, Parson's printing office and reading room and the county hall. Outside the school are six Bennett scholars, boys taken from the poor of Abingdon. These 'gown boys' are illustrated with their master, the Tesdale usher. Richard Parson's premises next door housed a stationer, bookseller and copper plate print shop with a subscription reading room upstairs and would have seen frequent use by Roysse's schoolboys. The Bennett Scholarships were established in 1608 by William and Ralph Bennett and the Tesdale Ushership in 1609 by Thomas Tesdale (who was also co-founder in 1624 of Pembroke College, Oxford, for the benefit of Abingdon school boys). Both Bennett Scholarships and the Tesdale Ushership came to an end in 1870 when the school moved to its present site adjacent to Albert Park.

St Helen's church, *c.* 1855. Viewed over the churchyard from Long Alley almshouses. Several almspeople are deep in conversation in the foreground with Mr Twitty's almshouses (1707) on the left and Brick Alley almshouses (1718) on the right.

Nag's Head Island, *c.* 1840. Timber is unloaded from a river barge and a partly loaded cart stands ready to take the logs to sawmills at the western end of the town or out to some of the neighbouring villages. St Helen's church with the malthouse lies over the river.

West St Helen Street, *c*. 1840. Conversation in front of St Helen's church. Coal gas was manufactured in the town from 1835 and the large streetlight was likely to have been thus powered. The building to the right of St Helen's tower and adjacent to part of the churchyard is on a site to be occupied from 1855 until 1944 by a large clothing factory.

St Helen's Wharf, *c*. 1835. The cast iron bridge was erected by the Wilts & Berks Canal Company in 1824 (left). Beyond barges tied up at the wharf, are the former 'Almshouses over the water' (demolished 1884) and the county gaol of 1811. A partly covered passenger ferry makes a desultory crossing towards Andersey Island.

River traffic, c. 1855. A Thames barge approaches St Helen's wharf; the river was one of the town's highways of commerce. A tribute to the coal using economy are the numerous chimney stacks around St Helen's church spire. At Abingdon wharves Midland coal was unloaded, brought by way of the Oxford canal and Somerset coal by way of the Wilts & Berks canal.

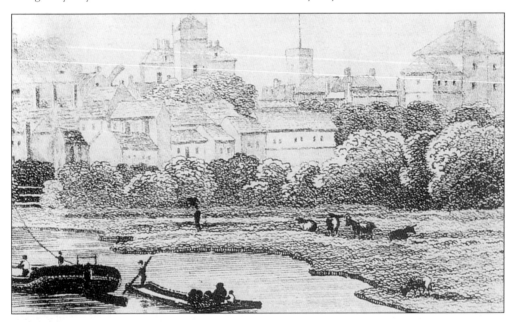

Abingdon, c. 1855. A town panorama is viewed from the river: the county hall, St Nicolas' church and county gaol. Sheep and cattle graze Andersey Island. The late Mr Ron Chung gave me these copies of old Abingdon prints in the late 1970s. Drawn just before the popularisation of photography the twelve prints offer an evocative picture of the mid-nineteenth century town.

Abingdon c. 1820. Men are at work on a couple of broad bottomed Thames barges close to the Wilts & Berks canal. A ferry, gondalier style, crosses from Andersey Island. The stone bridge over the river Ock was replaced by a cast iron bridge in 1824 from Acraman's of Bristol. At the southern end of this bridge for much of the nineteenth century was Gabriel Davis's iron works where canal and Thames barges were built and repaired. The business also made stern paddle-wheeled vessels that were used on the river Nile.

St Helen's wharf, c. 1820. This is similar to the 1815 painting by William Waite, a local artist, which hangs in the Hall of Christ's Hospital, but this illustration differs in a number of important details.

High Street, c. 1820. Shops with cast iron balconies are just recognisable in the street of today. The building standing in front of county hall at present accommodates Bragg's cycle shop.

High Street, c. 1855. Edwin Trendell's shop stands next to John Smith's haberdashery at the junction with West St Helen Street. Trendell was alderman and mayor of the borough, as well as master and governor of Christ's Hospital. He was also a benefactor of the town and traded as wholesale and retail grocer, tea dealer, tallow chandler, wine and brandy merchant. John Smith was the town's foremost linen and woollen draper, silk mercer and hatter.

Abingdon market cross. Abingdon's celebrated cross was destroyed by General Waller's Parliamentary troops in 1644. It rivalled Coventry cross and Bristol cross (now rebuilt at Stourhead) in quality and intricacy and was located close to today's county hall. This painting hangs in the Abbey room of the municipal buildings. There is a further painting of the cross, possibly by Sampson Strong of Oxford, sheltered on the outside wall of Long Alley almshouses.

Abingdon, 1793. This view of the town looking along Thames Street to the end of Abingdon Bridge, was drawn by C. Rosenberg. St Helen's church and the masts of a couple of Thames barges form the background.

Abingdon, 1793. An idealised view of Culham Bridge by C. Rosenberg, with a glimpse over Andersey Island to St Helen's church.

Market Place, c. 1900. Queen Victoria's golden jubilee statue (1887) looks over streets empty of traffic. St Nicolas' church, the Abbey gateway, guildhall and county hall fringe her view.

Two
Christ's Hospital

Christ's Hospital, 1890. Henry Taunt journeyed the Thames by boat to capture this early morning scene. Long Alley almshouses and Christ's Hospital Hall (1446) enclose St Helen's churchyard, with Brick Alley almshouses (1718) on the right.

Tomkins' almshouses, c. 1880. Endowed by Joseph Tomkins in 1731 by a bequest of property, these eight almshouses were built in Ock Street for elderly members of the Baptist community.

Opposite: Christ's Hospital, c. 1880. One of two unnamed and undated pencil sketches, this records Mr Twitty's almshouses, founded in 1707 by Charles Twitty, a native of Abingdon.

Christ's Hospital, c. 1960. The garden front of Long Alley was built in 1446. The Hall's ornamental lantern roof was added in 1707. The rubble-faced river front is fifteenth century but carries the date 1674.

Mr Twitty's almshouses, c. 1960. Charles Twitty left £1,700 (in 1706) as an endowment to be managed by the vicar and churchwardens of St Helen's to maintain in meat, drink and apparel, and all other necessaries of life, three poor aged men and three poor aged women. Born in Abingdon, Twitty became Deputy Auditor of the Exchequer and governor and benefactor of St Margaret's Hospital, Westminster.

Christ's Hospital, c. 1960. This is the east front of Long Alley facing St Helen's churchyard. Erected in 1446, the porch was added in 1605 and the lantern over the Hall in 1707. The Master and Governors have for centuries held their monthly meeting in the Hall, the former Guild of the Holy Cross pre-dated Christ's Hospital and met in the upper room above St Helen's church north porch.

Brick Alley almshouses, c. 1960. Erected in 1718 for eighteen almsmen and women it reputedly replaced an earlier almshouse built prior to 1417 by Geoffrey Barbour, one of the builders of Abingdon Bridge. Barbour intended his almshouse to be a place of shelter for the homeless poor to take refuge. Rebuilding was completed by 1720 and cost £632. Excellent workmanship was provided by Samuel Westbrooke, mason, and Charles Etty, carpenter, two skilled Abingdon tradesmen who also worked on Mr Twitty's almshouses.

Christ's Hospital, 1939. *The Times* newspaper published photographs of the almsmen and women and gave Christ's Hospital an album of the images. (Copyright *The Times*)

Christ's Hospital, 1939. Matron helps residents in the western garden of Long Alley. The clothing factory's gaunt outline, which was destroyed by fire in 1944, can be seen in the background. (Copyright: *The Times*)

Christ's Hospital, 1939. A kettle boils on the hob of a small kitchen range while this lady gets on with some personal washing. Around the room are family pictures and mementos. (Copyright: *The Times*)

Abingdon Bridge, 1964. Looking upstream from St Helen's Wharf this was once the site of the Almshouses over the water until demolished in 1884. Abingdon Bridge, partly rebuilt in 1928, is locally known as Burford Bridge, a corruption of Borough Ford, which it replaced in 1416 better to link Abingdon with London.

St Helen's church, c. 1960. The church is wider than it is long, having five aisles. On the south the outermost aisle is known as the Reade aisle of 1539. The neighbouring fourth aisle is called St Katherine's aisle. Christ's Hospital governors attending church sat here 'as in th' accustomed manner in tyme past'. Almspeople were placed 'in the nether part' of the same aisle.

St Helen's church spire, *c.* 1960. A steeple was added to the tower in the mid-fifteenth century, then rebuilt around 1662 and again in 1885. The spire was rebuilt in memory of George Louis Monck Gibbs of Clifton Hampden and the top portion of the old spire was placed in the churchyard west of Mr Twitty's Almshouse.

Park Crescent, 1960. The insignia of Christ's Hospital is seen at Whitefield, built in 1871 as part of the Victorian development on Christ's Hospital land around Albert Park. Whitefield was the home of Arthur E. Preston, FSA (1852-1942), historian of Christ's Hospital, Roysse's School, St Nicolas' church, and munificent benefactor of the town.

St Michael's church, 1890. Designed by Sir George Gilbert Scott and consecrated in January 1867, St Michael's was built on Christ's Hospital land acquired by Revd Nathaniel Dobson, vicar of Abingdon (1824-67). Harry Redfern (1861-1950), architect, designed the high altar (see pages 31 and 37).

Albert Park, 1890. The statue of Prince Albert was unveiled by Montague Bertie, 5th Earl of Abingdon, High Steward of the Borough, on 22 June 1865. The *Illustrated London News* carried details and a full-page illustration of the ceremony. John Gibbs of Oxford designed the forty-eight feet high, Box limestone and Mansfield sandstone statue. The seven-foot effigy of Albert is Portland stone. Christ's Hospital recreation ground was re-named Albert Park following his death in 1861 and completed in 1862. In June of that year Oliver Kilby was appointed first park keeper at £40 a year 'to keep the said ground in order', aided by a mower and a donkey.

Three

School

Abingdon School, 1827. This exterior view is from an engraving by J.C. Buckler in *Views of the Endowed Grammar Schools of England*. The headmaster's house is on the right with the schoolroom in the centre. The school was re-founded in 1563 by John Roysse, Abingdonian and Mercer of the City of London, to educate sixty-three scholars. The room measured sixty-three feet in length and was re-endowed in the sixty-third year of Roysse's life.

Abingdon School, 1793. The school yard as seen in Augustus Grafton's copy of 1844 of J. Smith's original drawing. Grafton's copy is in the possession of the school.

Schoolroom, 1841. This lithograph was drawn by Thomas G. Owen, MAS, assistant master at the school. Owen was a clever draughtsman and trained as an architect later practising at Abingdon and Maidenhead. The headmaster is seated (left) below the library gallery. The three masters, seated at desks facing him, taught English, French and mathematics. Seated facing the Eagle lectern, presented by Brasenose College (1743), is the Tesdale Usher (right) with six gowned Bennett Boys in his charge. Above the Usher hangs the school's Act of Parliament clock.

The school clock, 1964. This was given in 1743 by the Revd Thomas Woods (headmaster 1716-53), the most successful eighteenth-century head. This Act of Parliament clock, inscribed *Pereunt et Imputantur* (the hours perish and are recorded) a line taken from a poem by Martial, was transferred to the present buildings. The clock keeps good time in the Grundy Library.

Park Road, *c.* 1899. The school lodge was designed by Abingdonian architect Harry Redfern (see pages 27 and 31) and opened in 1897. In Abingdon Redfern restored the Roysse Room (1911), designed the high altar at St Michael's church, and completed work at Lacies Court, Bath Street, and Malthouse at St Helen's Wharf. He also designed laboratories at Cambridge and restored parts of Christ's College and Magdalene College. At Oxford he worked at Oriel College and St John's College and designed the university biochemistry laboratories. Redfern was also responsible for numerous public house designs in the Carlisle area.

Park Road, 1868. Edwin Dolby's front elevation of the new grammar school which opened in 1870 under the Revd Edgar Summers (headmaster 1870-83). Edwin Dolby (1838-1900) operated from architect's offices at 14 Park Crescent and London designing many houses around Albert Park. He was architect to the Wantage Tramway Company, rebuilt Garford church, added the south porch at Drayton and restored Kingston Bagpuize church. Dolby may have designed for Morland & Co, the Queen's Hotel, which formerly stood in Abingdon market place.

Thomas Teasdale (1547-1610), principal founder of Pembroke College, Oxford. Tesdale left £5,000 to educate Abingdon school boys at Oxford, initially and abortively at Balliol College, but latterly by re-founding Broadgates Hall as Pembroke College in 1624. He also founded the school's Tesdale Ushership for a master to teach the six poor Bennett Scholars by making a bequest of land and tithes at Upton in Warwickshire to pay their stipends. The scheme was managed by Christ's Hospital, Abingdon and this portrait hangs in the Hospital Hall.

A Bennett Scholar, 1840. William Bennett founded scholarships for six poor Abingdon boys to attend the grammar school. The 'Bennett Boys' wore gowns of cloth with a silver badge on the left side bearing the motto 'Master Bennett's Scholars' and a raised red cross with the date 1608. Entitled to free education for six years they were instructed by a special master in English, writing and accounts, had complete clothing twice a year, a mince pie and ten shillings annually on St Thomas's Day, £50 on leaving school as an apprenticeship fee to respectable trades or professions, £5 for clothing for each of two years after apprenticeship and preference for election to Abingdon scholarships at Pembroke College under Thomas Tesdale's will.

Abingdon School, 1867. This school group is pictured in front of the headmaster's house in the school yard. Six 'gown boys – the fancy six', scholars under William Bennett's bequest are clearly visible. Others wear a variety of headdress: bowlers, boaters, peaked industrial caps. Behind the headmaster and Tesdale Usher are several other masters and some seventy boys.

Two Abingdon Beaks, 1867. Pictured are headmaster, the Revd Dr William Alder Strange, DD, (headmaster 1840-68), an old boy of the school, and his Tesdale Usher, the Revd Edmund Tristram Horatio Harper (usher 1855-70, acting-headmaster 1868-70) both of Pembroke College. Dr Strange retired from the last headship at the town centre school to become vicar of Bishop Middleham, Durham (1868-74). The Revd Edmund Harper, the last Tesdale Usher, became vicar of Luddington in North Lincolnshire in 1871, where he remained until his death aged ninety-seven years in 1923.

Dr W.A. Strange, 1883. One of two portraits of William Alder Strange (1830-74) at the school. H.J. Brooks painted this portrait, by subscription of the old boys in 1883, nine years after Dr Strange's death and fifteen years after he had resigned the headship.

Abingdon School 1st IV, 1881. From left: M.I. Baker (cox), F.J. Wadham (stroke), F.P. Lysaght (3), J.B. Reeves (2), H.M. Digby (bow), outside Abingdon School Rowing Club's boat house then on Wilsham Road. This successful crew retained the Town Trophy at Abingdon Regatta first won by the school in 1880. The last Abingdon Regatta for many years was held in 1882.

Abingdon School 1st IV, 1882. They were winners of the Town Fours at the Abingdon Regatta. From left: J.B. Reeves, G.H. Morland, W.A.deB. Corry, H.M. Digby and, seated, M.I. Baker.

Abingdon School 1st IV, 1897. From left: H.F. Gale (cox), H.E. Johnson (stroke), A.J.T. McCreery (3), W.B. Collingwood (2), W.M. Austin (bow). The main race at the school regatta in July 1897 was against the Old Abingdonian Rowing Club. 'Unfortunately bow of the Old Boys' crew lost his oar at the start of the race and the School rowed over easily.'

Abingdon School Regatta, c. 1900. Nattily attired spectators watch the start of races above old Culham Bridge and the wooden footbridge spanning Swift Ditch. The clergyman sitting on the bank (right) is believed to be the Venerable Henry Rudge Hayward (1831-1912), Archdeacon of Cirencester and Canon Residentiary of Gloucester, an old Abingdonian who came from a well-known Wantage family. Hayward was a successful oarsman at both Abingdon and Pembroke College.

The Revd Edgar Summers, BD, (1834-1907), c. 1884. Summers was the first headmaster (1870-83) of the new school. He came to Abingdon with a double first from Trinity College, Cambridge in Classics and Theology, experience as second master at Bury St Edmunds Grammar School (1859-62) and as assistant master at Brighton College (1862-1870). Under Summers the school prospered. Out of private resources he purchased part of Lacies Court on behalf of the school and later helped establish the Young & Summers scholarship in mathematics. He was preferred to the incumbency of Brading in the Isle of Wight in 1883 retiring in 1906. He died at Winchester the following year.

Corn Exchange, 1910. Furniture, flowers and potted palms are arranged for school prize giving by Dr J.P. Postgate, Professor of Latin at the University of Liverpool and Fellow of Trinity College, Cambridge. The Corn Exchange, designed by Charles Bell in 1886, stood facing the Market Place but was demolished in the 1960s to make way for the Bury shopping precinct.

Abingdon School day boys, 1874. Back row from left: Hugh Taylor, F.W. Reed, W.J. Smith, James Rant, A. Challenor, G.W. Griffith, Louis Davis, F. Bryan, E.J. Stokes, S. Taylor. Third row: J.E. Kimber, J.G.T. West, J. Tomkins, F. Chaplin, Herbert Comins, F.I. Comins, H.G.W. D'Almaine, G.W. Shepherd, J. Harris, R.H. Nicholls. Second row: W.M. Abbott, F.C. Bayliss, Harry Redfern, W.B. Ball, E.P. Blagrove, H.W. Harding, H.S. Challenor, W. Smith, W. Ballard, W.H. Tayler. Front row: C. Hemming, W.W. Smee, E. Ivey, J.M. Townsend, E.W. Johnson, H. Clinch, T.H. Witham, W.F. Young, W. Pitt, H.G.S. Sykes. The six remaining Bennett scholars wear mortarboards and gowns (see page 33). Louis Davis (1860-1941) became a watercolourist and glass artist and has been denominated the last member of the Arts & Crafts movement. Harry Redfern (1861-1950) became a London architect (see pages 27 and 31). J.G.T. West (1860-1931) was a pupil of Edwin Dolby the Abingdon architect, (see page 108).

Abingdon, 1890. The school gate about which *Jackson's Oxford Journal* (1811) says: 'we are informed that the (4th) Earl of Abingdon, High Steward of the Borough…has also presented to them £100, for the purpose of defraying the expence of the Gothic gateway on entering the School-yard.' Above the gateway are carved the arms of John Roysse, the school's re-founder, the Borough of Abingdon and the Abbey.

Park Crescent, 1972. Mrs Margaret Thatcher, Education Secretary is pictured with W.E.K. Anderson (headmaster 1970-75), having turned the first sod for the new dining hall. Mrs Thatcher went on to be Prime Minister (1979-87). Eric Anderson in turn became headmaster of Shrewsbury School, Eton College, rector of Lincoln College, Oxford, and is currently Provost of Eton. Three masters stand on the right: Rodney MacKinnon (now a judge), Chris Owen (latterly headmaster of John Mason School, Abingdon) and Martin Blocksidge (director of studies, St Dunstan's College, London).

Michael St John Parker, 1995. Michael Parker (headmaster 1975-2001) came to Abingdon after teaching at King's School, Canterbury and Winchester College. He oversaw substantial advances in school buildings and academic attainment.

Visit of Lady Thatcher, 1994. Lady Thatcher inspected Mercer's Court and gave an address in the Amey Hall. She is seen here with the school prefects, from left: James McCormick, Kuberan Pushparajah, Alexander Davis, Adam Guy, Kingsley Jones, Lady Thatcher, Philip Baker, James Sporle, Ben Uttenthal, Rowan Browne and, partly hidden, Hugh Gittins.

The Guest Room, Our Lady's Convent, Abingdon, Berkshire.

Our Lady's Convent, 1930. The convent guest room. The author recalls being interviewed in this room in 1946 by the impressive Reverend Mother, upon the basis of which he entered the boys' junior school under Sister Catherine, a splendid teacher, who in due course became herself the Reverend Mother.

Drayton, c. 1885. Mrs Deacon ran a private school largely for girls at Lime Close but with a number of boys. Mrs Deacon was operating the school in 1854. By 1891, aged eighty-four she still acted as the school's dame. It may be Mrs Deacon standing on the far right.

Conduit Road, 1960. Trinity (Wesleyan) Methodist school, situated adjacent to the church, opened in 1875 to the design of J. Woodman and was much influenced by John Creemer Clarke, town clothing manufacturer. He was mayor of Abingdon, 1870, Master of Christ's Hospital and Liberal MP for Abingdon, 1874-85.

Hanney National School, 1906. Pictured are a group of well turned-out children of this school, which was established in 1846 for 120 pupils. By 1906 the school ran under the headship of H. Leslie Edwardes (headmaster 1896-1928) who imprinted his distinctive character and style of discipline on the school. Of the fourteen boys all of whom were eligible to serve in the First World War, Edwardes wrote in the school log book for July 1915, 'One hundred and seventeen village lads have offered themselves for service in his Majesty's Forces out of a population of less that seven hundred.' Twenty-nine Hanney men died in that war.

Four
Moving Around

Abingdon, c. 1910. A bumpy St Helen's church outing in two solid-tyred City of Oxford charabancs. Men fill the first coach with just a few men seated behind the women in the second coach. The three lads in front were destined to be left at home.

Buckland, c. 1910. One of the several village shops, displaying provisions on the pavement. The pony-trap contrasts starkly with the chauffeur-driven car parked beyond the shop – possibly driven down from Buckland House to collect groceries.

Buckland, c. 1934. The blacksmith and wheelwright's workshop provided repair facilities for the village's horse-drawn vehicles. Now demolished, the building was located on the northern side of today's memorial hall car park. Standing with hammer slung over a shoulder is Charles Turner.

Charney Bassett, *c.* 1920. Edward Alfred Hammond (1872-1944) had been coachman to an English family in Paris. When they wished to use a car Mr Hammond declined to be chauffeur and returned to England eventually settling at Charney Bassett. In his garage he housed this pony and tubb that Mrs Hammond would drive and which is seen here in New Road. The Hammond family in due course acquired a smart new Citroen. Pony and tubb were then used solely for pleasure outings.

Abingdon, c. 1930. Daniel Trotman and assistants delivering bread in a somewhat unevenly balanced delivery cart. At this period Abingdon had numerous scattered bakeries. Housewives would favour one or another according to the flavour, texture and style of their bread. Trotman's tasty wholemeal cobs were with some much favoured.

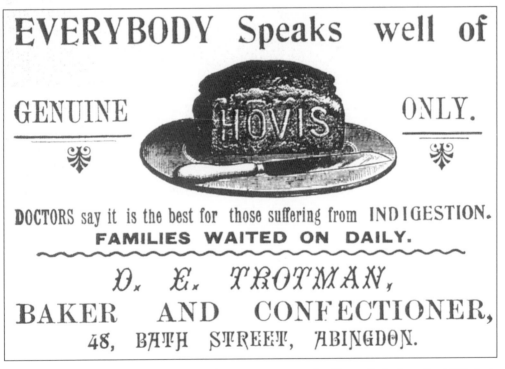

EVERYBODY Speaks well of

GENUINE   HOVIS   ONLY.

DOCTORS say it is the best for those suffering from INDIGESTION.
FAMILIES WAITED ON DAILY.

D. E. TROTMAN,
BAKER AND CONFECTIONER,
48, BATH STREET, ABINGDON.

Trotman's bakery, 1920. Located in Bath Street opposite the Horse & Jockey. By 1950 their premises were in Ock Street adjacent to the Regent cinema. When Freda and Jessie Trotman gave up business, Holmes & Son's bakery, which had been further down Ock Street, took over the Trotman bakery and tea room.

Hanney church choir outing, *c. 1920*. Arrival at the pier head, Bournemouth, in this solid-tyred South Midland charabanc. From the right, front: Sidney Barrett, the Revd F.H. Noon (vicar 1915-27), H. Leslie Edwardes (headmaster 1896-1928). Row one: Cleeve Higgs, Frank Bunce, Albert Tombs, Bob Breakspear, Jim Bunce. Row two: Billy Cox, Charlie Cox, Eric Cox, and Harry Cox. Row three: Fred Daubney, Vic Lamble, George Burnett, Cyril Barrow, and George Belcher. Row four, standing: Wilf Barrow, Ted Bunce, Ernie Lamble, John Broughton, Billy Spindloe, Len Clinch. Sitting from right: Jack Barrett, Butty Adams, Bob Cowie, Ned Shepherd, Eric Fisher, Eddy Tarry (see page 89).

Punting on the river, 1811. Serving as a ferry from a Thames Street inn or for fishing on the mill stream, the engraving by W. Cooke indicates the usea of the river as highway. Drawn by S. Owen, it shows the newly built county gaol with St Helen's spire behind one of the narrow medieval portions of Abingdon Bridge.

Wilts & Berks canal, c. 1880. The canal opened to Abingdon in 1810, closed by 1906 and was abandoned around 1914. This lifting bridge near Abingdon is reminiscent of Caldecott Bridge close to the basin and dock at the eastern end of the waterway. The canal was intended to bring coal from the Somerset coalfield by way of the Somerset Coal canal, the Kennet & Avon, and from Semington on the Wilts & Berks to the towns and villages of the Vale of the White Horse, undercutting the cost of coal transported to Abingdon from the Midlands by way of the Oxford canal and River Thames.

Wilts & Berks canal, *c.* 1920. Tithe Farm bridge takes the Abingdon to Drayton road over the canal. The prominent tree to the right stood beside Caldecott Road in a corner of Ladygrove House. The notice (right) from the *County of Berks* is a warning 'to traction engine drivers and others'.

Wilts & Berks canal, *c.* 1920. Caldecott Road (right) runs to its junction with Drayton Road, then the main Birmingham to Southampton road. This boatered man surveys a view that is now in the centre of south Abingdon's housing development.

Abingdon Station, 1910. A branch line from Radley was opened on 2 June 1856 by the Abingdon Railway Company as broad gauge track. It was taken over by the Great Western Railway in 1904 and closed to passenger traffic in 1961.

Abingdon station, 23 July 1963. A special train transported Abingdon School to Coventry during celebration of the school's Quatercentenary year. Some of the six hundred members of school and staff are waiting on the platform. Headboarded 'The Abingdonian', the train consequently left Abingdon some two years after the station closed to passenger traffic. At Coventry Cathedral the school choir sang Evensong. Could this be the last passenger train ever to leave Abingdon Station?

Abingdon station, *c.* 1960. A train for Radley passes some of the town's malthouses.

Radley station, *c.* 1920. The *Bunk*, as the Abingdon train was called, leaves on its two-and-a-half mile journey to Abingdon pulled by tank engine No. 2537.

Avro E 500, 1916. This aircraft, owned by the Holmes brothers of East Hanney, is a single-seater Avro biplane developed in 1911 and adopted by the Royal Flying Corps. John Holmes runs behind the aircraft. It competed for the Mortimer Singer Naval Prize, an early flying competition. Sir Mortimer Singer, KBE (of sewing machine fame) made his home at Milton Hill House, took British citizenship and was awarded his knighthood in recognition for services during the First World War when he gave over his house as a military hospital (see page 127).

East Hanney, 1916. Piloted by Lt John Holmes, this was the first aeroplane ever to land in the village, on 26 October 1916. In a letter dated June 1978, which has only recently come to light, John Holmes writes to Oswald Barrett, son of John Parker Barrett the builder of West Hanney: 'I thought you might be interested and amused with this old snap of your father's backview, examining the aeroplane I flew to Hanney on 26 October 1916, sixty-two years ago. It was taken by my father [James Robins Holmes, 1859-1938] and landed in Mrs Stevenson's field by Pound Croft on the Steventon Road. A long time ago!' At the time of writing John Holmes was eighty years old and rather arthritic.

Avro E 500, 1916. The Holmes brothers stand in front of their aircraft. A tweed-suited onlooker, smoking a cigarette, holds the propeller while somewhat recklessly standing next to a jerrycan of fuel and in close range of the aircraft's engine and fuel tanks.

Frederick James Vernon Holmes (1896-1967), 1916. The Holmes brothers were early aviators with something of their father's courage, business flair and pioneering spirit. Under them aircraft assembly work took place in a barn east of the village at Yew Tree Farm on the Steventon Road. Fred Holmes allegedly asked his father for funding to help along their aircraft project but was told: 'I had to start from scratch. You can start from scratch', but J.R. Holmes allowed his sons to rent Lower Mill, East Hanney, for assembly work.

John Duncan Vernon Holmes (1898-1980), 1916. John Holmes together with his elder brother Frederick formed the Berkshire Aviation Company. It was their father J.R. Holmes, who as village photographer took the previous photograph (see page 52). J.R. Holmes, entrepreneur, also developed a postal sales business in primitive contraceptive devices which he ran from the Mulberries in East Hanney (see page 90).

Five
The Berkshire Yeomanry
1900-1919

Berkshire Yeomanry, 1960. Each April veterans and their descendants have met at the memorial to Philip Wroughton on Woolley Downs to honour the memory of those who fought in the Yeomanry at Gallipoli and in Palestine.

D Squadron, 11 August 1914. Mobilization day. The squadron, which recruited from Abingdon and North Berkshire, parades in Wantage market place. The regiment served in an infantry role at Gallipoli as part of the 2nd Mounted Division under Major-Gen W.E. Peyton, CB. The second brigade comprised the Royal Bucks Hussars, Berkshire Yeomanry and Dorset Yeomanry. After Gallipoli D Squadron fought in Palestine.

Berkshire Yeomanry, 1911. Douglas Eady (1890-1968) in full uniform of the Royal Horse Artillery. He was the son of C.H. Eady, bailiff to Lord Wantage, and was a specialist breeder of Hereford cattle and unrivalled competition judge of shire-horses. After the First World War Douglas Eady farmed Church Farm, West Hanney.

East Hanney, 1919. This was the wedding of Douglas Eady to Sophia Dandridge, the East Hanney miller's daughter at the church of St James the less. The war had just ended and Douglas Eady wears his Berkshire Yeomanry uniform. Standing on the left in trilby hat is Robert (Bob) Pike (1893-1966), who for a short while farmed Rectory Farm, West Hanney, then for many years, Manor Farm, Lyford.

Berkshire Yeomanry. The cap badge and the officers' collar badge show a stylised horse after the ancient Uffington hill figure carved on White Horse Hill. The backing for the cap badge was a red oval.

Berkshire Yeomanry, 1914. The Yeomanry parade in Wallingford market place at the outbreak of war.

Berkshire Yeomanry, 1914. After the formal parade came the stand easy. Rifles are tripoded and horses fed from nosebags.

Queen's Own Oxfordshire Hussars, 1912. Troopers and NCOs of the Oxfordshire Hussars take a lunch break while on exercise during a field day. A couple of village lads look on from woodland beyond this picnic.

Berkshire Yeomanry, 1911. Douglas Eady firmly mounted on his alert and extremely well-polished hunter while in camp at Churn.

D Squadron, Berkshire Yeomanry, 1914. At the centre is Major Philip Wroughton (1888-1917). *The North Berks Herald* reported in April 1917 that he had been killed in action in Palestine aged twenty-nine years. He was the son of the late Philip Wroughton of Woolley Park. 'Had not military duties claimed his services... he would have succeeded his father in the public duties of the county, if not in Parliament. Philip Wroughton was a county Justice of the Peace, governor of Wantage Town Lands, governor of King Alfred's School as well as a prominent member of the Old Berks Hunt who rode in the Point-to-Point races. The young Squire had been previously in action with the Berkshire Yeomanry at Gallipoli, and was invalided home for a while.'

Summer camp at Churn, 1912. This postcard from Douglas Eady to his brother H. Norman Eady of Northampton reads: 'this photo of Sgt, Corporal, Bombardier and a gunner of our sub-section taken by my tent. Having an easy time but have had a lot of rain. Am writing this about four miles from camp, just halted, on a field day.'

Berkshire Royal Horse Artillery, Churn Camp, 1911. Douglas Eady writes home: 'Having a grand time for camp. What do you think of my photo? The three chaps on my left are in my tent and the other is two tents off.'

The Load of Mischief, 1913. Standing from left: Parker, Jenkins, Harding, Gerring. Kneeling: Miller, R. Whitfield, D. Eady, Telling. Sitting: Fowler, Clare, Moore, Quelch, Sell, Kendall.

Berkshire Yeomanry, 1911. Seven trumpeters dressed in No. 1 uniform at Churn Camp. In turn these were the men who may also have sounded by bugle, reveille, on parade and lights-out while in camp.

Berkshire Yeomanry, 1912. The machine gun section at Churn Camp. In front of the officer in charge, at the centre, is an effective (Bofors) machine gun and open ammunition box.

Berkshire Yeomanry, c. 1914. William Pryor of Harwell is pictured at a military establishment somewhere in England wearing *sola topi*, implying imminent departure for the Mediterranean and Gallipoli campaign. As part of the 2nd Mounted Brigade, this cavalryman stands in front of shoulder high racks for the temporary storage of saddles and bridles used while saddling up their horses.

Churn Camp, 1911. Bell tents act as sleeping accommodation for the men, in addition there is a mess tent and liquid refreshment tent. Officers' quarters are quite separate and surrounded by hurdles covered in straw. The Didcot to Newbury railway line and Churn Halt, which in summer transported up to two thousand troops to the camp, is visible top right. Outside the men's bell tents are numerous bicycles and half-a-dozen tethered horses.

William James Pryor, 1911. Formally dressed in Berkshire Yeomanry No. 1 uniform, William Pryor (1893-1968), here aged eighteen, is pictured at Montpellier, Harwell, by Warland Andrew of Abingdon (see page 86).

Berkshire Yeomanry, *c.* 1912. Standing from left: William Pryor, Harold Pryor (1894-1937), sitting: Francis Maggs, James Stibbs Napper (1893-1956), showing off their latest equipment, the Lee-Enfield 303 calibre rifle. All the weapons appear to be cocked, but one hopes the magazines are empty and safety catches on.

Berkshire Yeomanry, 1913. The winning D Squadron tug-of-war team was photographed while in camp at Churn. An enthusiastic note on this postcard from Wantage sent by Douglas Eady in July 1913 to his brother H.N. Eady at Northampton says: 'This is the team, we could pull anything, especially the afternoon this was taken…we are busy haymaking, have done more than half of it. Had the best camp I have ever been to.'

Churn camp, 1911. Sitting on the running board could be the owner and his chauffeur while visiting the Yeomanry at annual camp. Military men have taken over the car to have themselves photographed making a contrast with their usual mode of transport seen in the horses tethered in the background.

Churn camp, 1912. Early morning ablutions with men sharing a bucket of cold water for their wash, shave and brush up. Note the horse saddle in the foreground.

Churn camp, 1912. Standing: Lance Corporal William Pryor and Harold Pryor, both of Harwell. Sitting: Howard Maggs of Longcot and Jim Napper of East Hagbourne.

Berkshire Yeomanry, 1913. Included here are, standing left: William James Pryor and seated from left: Francis Maggs, Douglas Eady, -?-, Jim Napper.

One of the last postcards home, 15 April 1915. This was to Mr C.H. Eady, Lockinge (Bailiff to Lord Wantage) from his son Norman. 'We are getting lovely weather. Just passed some islands. Tonight can see some lights on the African coast. Supposed to reach Malta tomorrow. Have not seen anything of Douglas's boat [Douglas Eady, his brother] since they left Avonmouth, nor any of the other transport.' Norman Eady was killed August 20-22 1915 and was in the first list of Berkshire casualties from the Dardanelles.

Churn camp, 1911. Seated, from left: Pench Maggs, -?-, William Pryor. Standing: Harold Pryor, Jim Napper. Polished saddle and harness hang over the stand with six horses in the background.

Churn camp, 1913. From left: Jenkins, D. Eady, Timms (driving), Goodenough (of Prior's Court, West Hanney), Watts, Penfold.

Berkshire Yeomanry, 1913. Men of D Squadron in best uniform. From left: Harold Pryor, Jim Napper, William Pryor, Francis Maggs.

Cairo, June 1915. Four Hanney men of the Yeomanry were photographed in Egypt while on the way to fight at Gallipoli. Sitting, from left: Joseph Smith, Guy Smith. Standing: Robert Dandridge, Leonard Barrett. This postcard is from Leonard Barrett (posted Cairo, 28 June 1915) to Miss Nora Barnes of Cricklewood, London. After the war she married Leonard Barrett. He became a partner in J.P. Barrett & Co., builders of West Hanney. Bob Dandridge was killed three days after landing at Suvla Bay.

Bill Walters, *c.* 1915. Every inch a Sergeant, Walters, who became licensee of the Prince of Wales at Didcot Station, sits in front of a painted backdrop of potted palms, flowers and curtains. The Berkshire Yeomanry badge is clearly visible on his cap.

Churn camp, 1911. Three horse-drawn ammunition wagons. Douglas Eady in dark uniform, rides in front of the central wagon.

Berkshire Volunteers, c. 1881. T.E. Morland of West Ilsley House and of the family of local brewers, wrote to *Berkshire Life* in October 1956: 'Please accept my apologies for the poor condition of this photograph which I rescued from a dustbin. I believe it to be of a group of Berkshire Volunteers in camp at Lockinge in the 1880s. My grandfather, Edward Morland, of Abingdon, was a member of the Volunteers and he is standing fifth from the left.'

Berkshire Territorial Yeomanry, c. 1912. An Abingdon troop of sixteen troopers and their NCO stand easy while at camp at Bulford on Salisbury Plain.

Berkshire Yeomanry, 1911. Three
unnamed troopers in a temporary booth
at Churn that was set up by enterprising
photographers at summer camp.

Robert Dandridge (1899-1915). He
was the son of Alfred Dandridge,
miller at East Hanney. Young Bob
Dandridge arrived at Suvla Bay on 18
August 1915 with D squadron and
was in the first list of casualties from
the Dardanelles having been killed,
21 August 1915, aged sixteen years,
while taking part in the attack on
Scimitar Hill (Hill 70). This
photograph was taken at Christmas
1914, eight months before his death.
There is a memorial to him in the
south transept of West Hanney
church (see page 74).

Berkshire Yeomanry, 21 August 1915. Second Mounted Brigade (Berks, Bucks and Dorset Yeomanry) close to the beach at Lala Baba before the disastrous Battles of Chocolate and Scimitar Hills. The case in the foreground (right) bears a cross and the name Arthur Groom Parham. In 1915 the Revd A.G. Parham was temporary chaplain to the Forces attached to the 2nd Mounted Division. By 1919 he was Deputy Assistant Chaplain General with a Military Cross and two mentions in dispatches. After the war he became rector of Easthampstead (1921-26), vicar of St Mary's, Reading (1926-46), Archdeacon of Berkshire from 1942 and Bishop of Reading. Having attended Magdalen College School, Parham knew the Abingdon area intimately and retired from his ministry to Little Wittenham.

Six
Trade and Business

Abingdon carpet factory, *c.* 1900. Men work the carpet looms: and a selection of newly made carpets, rugs and cord squares hang over stands on the left. At the centre a woman finishes and checks a rug, while in the distance the factory foreman in bowler hat has his hands firmly thrust into his pockets.

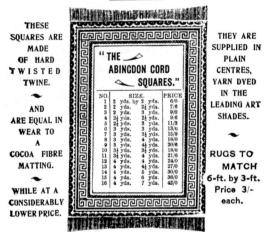

THE STRONGEST CARPET MADE
FOR
— • HARD WEAR. • —
The HEAVIEST and the CHEAPEST.
Registered "REVIREDIS" Trade Mark.

THESE
SQUARES ARE
MADE
OF HARD
TWISTED
TWINE.

~

AND
ARE EQUAL IN
WEAR TO
A
COCOA FIBRE
MATTING.

~

WHILE AT A
CONSIDERABLY
LOWER PRICE.

"THE
ABINGDON CORD
SQUARES."

NO.	SIZE.		PRICE
1	2 yds. by 2	yds.	6/0
2	2 yds.	2¼ yds.	7/6
3	2 yds.	3 yds.	9/0
4	2¼ yds.	2¼ yds.	9/6
5	2¼ yds.	3 yds.	11/3
6	3 yds.	3 yds.	13/6
7	3 yds.	3¼ yds.	15/9
8	3 yds.	4 yds.	18/0
9	3 yds.	4¼ yds.	20/6
10	3½ yds.	3½ yds.	18/6
11	3½ yds.	4 yds.	21/6
12	4 yds.	4 yds.	24/0
13	4 yds.	4½ yds.	27/0
14	4 yds.	5 yds.	30/0
15	4 yds.	6 yds.	36/0
16	4 yds.	7 yds.	42/0

THEY ARE
SUPPLIED IN
PLAIN
CENTRES,
YARN DYED
IN THE
LEADING ART
SHADES.

~

RUGS TO
MATCH
6-ft. by 3-ft.
Price 3/-
each.

SEAMLESS, REVERSIBLE, ~
~ ECONOMICAL, ORNAMENTAL.

Copied from *Furniture and Decoration and the Furniture Gazette* of March 1st, 1894.
"THE 'ABINGDON' CORD SQUARES:—
"For thorough hard wear, for Economy, and for Artistic appearance, there
is no Carpet at present on the market that can surpass Messrs. Shepherd Bros.'
'Abingdon' Squares."

Abingdon carpet factory, c. 1890. Men and some women workers at the riverside sacking, matting and carpet factory, built in 1856, which extended over part of the island site above Abingdon Bridge. Latterly it was occupied also by the town's gas works and now by the Upper Reaches Hotel.

Abingdon cord squares, 1894. A price list for Abingdon carpets and *Abingdon Cord Squares* made by the Shepherd brothers. The Shepherd family built the house now known as Glyndowr in Park Crescent in 1881 as a highly ornamental dwelling in bright red, white and blue brick with a decorative tower to make it the highest building in the town. In many ways the house is quite out of keeping with the style of surrounding properties, as if partly to make a statement about their wealth gained from manufacturing.

Abingdon tannery, c. 1910. Eleven women workers strip the fleece from sheepskins. Skins and fleeces hang behind awaiting their attention with a bundle of fleeces on the right. This was dirty work employing a high proportion of women in unpleasant conditions. Apart from an apron the women wear little protective clothing.

Abingdon tannery, c. 1910. Stripping a fleece with a whole series of fleeces racked behind waiting for work upon them. This dirty and smelly occupation was a major employer of Abingdon's female labour force.

Abingdon, 1960. The malthouse of Joseph Tomkins. Part of Abingdon's prosperity was built on malting and the malt trade but both have now disappeared from the town. So too has the Tomkins family. In 1899 C.A. Pryce, solicitor, bought the malthouse for £822 to convert to a private residence: Harry Redfern, architect, may have redesigned it (see page 33). By 1945 the malthouse came to the Ministry of Supply and 1948-63 it was used by AERE Harwell then by Culham College to house students.

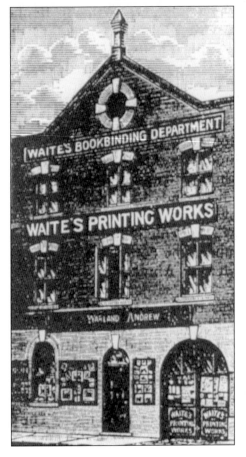

Waite's bookbinding and printing works, 1900. In Stert Street next to St Nicolas' church, this enterprise was on the site of today's branch of Lloyds TSB Bank. Warland Andrew's photographic studio was formerly located on part of the ground floor with Waite's print works thundering around him.

Hooke's printing works, 1905. William Holden Hooke (1864-1937) moved from Guildford to run this printing business in Abingdon initially on the site of Waite's print works and with a shop in the Market Place. It was developed by his youngest son, John Holden Hooke (1907-1988), as the Abbey Press, in premises of the former Picture Palace in Stert Street.

Beesley's of Abingdon, 1905. The shop in High Street may have the pedigree of a mercer's enterprise extending back to 1673. After William Beesley and E.H. Beesley, Oswald Barrett and his wife Gladys, then their son David Barrett owned the general outfitter's business. Oswald Barrett started work in 1908 as E.H. Beesley's apprentice and finished his time as owner. In a newspaper interview in 1969 he recalled: 'in the early days you could get a shirt for 1s and a three-piece suit for not much more than 12s.'

Coxeter's, Ock Street, *c.* 1895. Wholesale ironmongers, bicycle manufacturers and repairers. Charles Coxeter founded the business in 1836. This building became, until 2001, Beadle's of Abingdon, ironmongers and locksmiths, which business moved to the shop after the Coxeter brothers crossed Ock Street to a range of buildings now demolished for the entry to Stratton Way. After the war Cyril and Wilfred Coxeter presided over the store that offered a veritable magpie's nest of goods for the country housewife, ranging from furniture to lengths of silk to pudding basins.

Ock Street, c. 1908. Only horse drawn traffic is visible in the street, but there are two signs for Abingdon cycles and motors at two of Coxeters' shops, one on the right, and for motor cars opposite. Further along are the premises of Coxeter & Andrew.

Abingdon, c. 1930. The MG car company occupied the former Pavlova Leather factory off Spring Road in 1929. It made Abingdon well known worldwide through its competitions department and by sales of MGs, especially in the transatlantic market.

Vineyard, 1947. Fred Stimpson's fruit, vegetable and confectionery shop at 94 The Vineyard. The shop was opened 31 March 1946, to serve the northern part of the town in premises that had been Tom Dix's cycle shop.

Ock Street, 1939. Fred Stimpson's general store at 149 Ock Street was used as an air-raid warden's post. Local wardens were to report here at the first alert prior to sounding the town's air-raid siren as a general warning to the townspeople.

Abingdon cattle market, c. 1970. As Berkshire's county town until 1869, Abingdon was pre-eminently an agricultural centre with three separate markets for sheep in the Square, pigs in Bath Street and cattle in front of county hall. The three markets were consolidated behind the corn exchange (demolished) near the site of the Bury shopping centre. With redevelopment in the 1960s the livestock market was rebuilt east of Stert Street. Abingdon now has no livestock market.

Shepherd's hardware store, 1905. Goods advertised for sale at this town centre shop attest to the agricultural nature of Abingdon business. To sell such a mixture of agricultural and domestic appliances from premises in one of the town's prime shopping streets would from today's perspective perhaps seem extraordinary.

SHEPHERD'S HARDWARE STORES

Agency for all the leading

IMPLEMENT MAKERS.

Plough Shares & Fittings always in Stock,

Manufactured by RANSOME'S, HOWARD'S, etc.

FOOD PREPARING MACHINERY FITTED UP WITH SHAFTING, &c.

Turnip Cutters, Pulpers, Cake & Oat Crushers, Chaff Cutters, &c.

ESTIMATES GIVEN FOR LIGHTING AND HEATING

OIL, GAS,

CHURCHES,　　　　　　　　　　　　　　GREEN-

CHAPELS,　　　　　　　　　　　　　　HOUSES,

SCHOOLS,　　　　　　　　　　　　　　HALLS,

DWELLINGS,　　　　AND　　　　　　SHOPS.

HOT WATER.

Laundries fitted up for Steam Power, etc.

ADDRESS:—

SHEPHERD, High St., Abingdon, Berks.

Morland & Co. brewers of fine ales, 1711-2000. John Morland purchased the West Ilsley Brewery from Benjamin Smith in 1711, which Edward Henry Morland inherited in 1855. Edward Morland then took over Eagle brewery (1861) together with Abbey brewery (1866) forming United Breweries, Abingdon.

Abbey brewery, c. 1850. Edward Child was proprietor in 1779. Brewing ceased at Abingdon in 2000 following Greene King's takeover of Morland & Co. In the extensive Morland family were two artists: Henry Robert Morland (1716-1797) and George Morland (1763-1804), a connection commemorated in the Morland & Co. logo.

East St Helen Street, *c. 1960.* Pictured is the King's Head and Bell. *Inns and Alehouses of Abingdon, 1550-1978* says that this pub 'could justifiably claim to be one of the oldest…in Abingdon…recorded in 1554.' Throughout the eighteenth century it was known as the King's Head and Bell, but sometime in the nineteenth century became simply the Bell or Old Bell. By the twentieth century, however, it had reverted to its former name. The king's head is that of Charles I, who is believed to have held a council of war in the building when Abingdon was in royalist hands.

Market Place, *c. 1920.* The Abbey Café is on the left next door to a shop selling an unusual mixture of fruit, confectionery and tobacco which is on the site of today's Bragg's cycle shop. Home and Colonial, the grocer, is at the corner of High Street and Market Place.

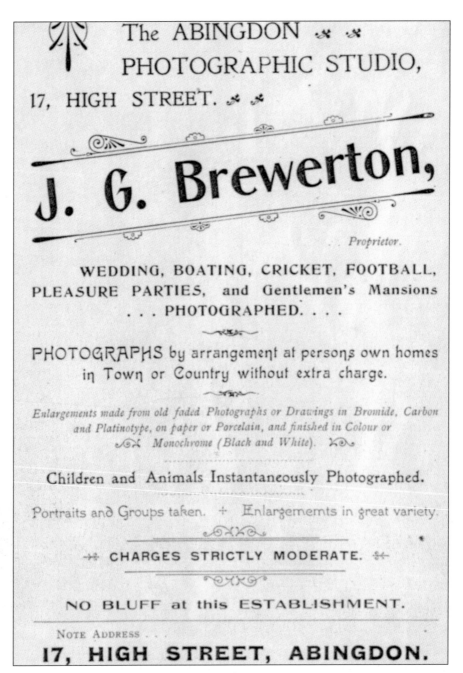

The ABINGDON ✄ ✄
PHOTOGRAPHIC STUDIO,
17, HIGH STREET. ✄ ✄

J. G. Brewerton,

. . . *Proprietor.*

WEDDING, BOATING, CRICKET, FOOTBALL,
PLEASURE PARTIES, and Gentlemen's Mansions
. . . PHOTOGRAPHED. . . .

PHOTOGRAPHS by arrangement at persons own homes
in Town or Country without extra charge.

*Enlargements made from old faded Photographs or Drawings in Bromide, Carbon
and Platinotype, on paper or Porcelain, and finished in Colour or
Monochrome (Black and White).*

Children and Animals Instantaneously Photographed.

Portraits and Groups taken.   +   Enlargememts in great variety.

✄ CHARGES STRICTLY MODERATE. ✄

NO BLUFF at this ESTABLISHMENT.

NOTE ADDRESS . . .
17, HIGH STREET, ABINGDON.

Abingdon, 1908. Photography had become increasingly popular by the start of the twentieth century and the town had several studios. Warland Andrew's Thameside studio was in Stert Street, next to St Nicolas' church. He does not seem to have advertised in the town but was 'patronised by royalty' (see page 113). W.J. Vasey at 14-16 Broad Street was more explicit: 'patronized by HM The King and HM The Emperor of Germany, etc. etc'. A further exponent of the art, Henry J. Brooks, had been in business as photographer, bookseller and artist in the Market Place. J.G. Brewerton's studio in High Street, in what must have become a tight market, advertised in contrast to his rivals: 'no bluff at this establishment.'

Seven
People

Bath Street, c. 1910. A smoking party is pictured on Lacies Court lawn. Only two faces have been identified, seated eleventh from left is E.H. Beesley, proprietor of the outfitter's shop in High Street and Oswald Barrett is standing behind him. Oswald became his son-in-law and eventually took over the business (see page 79). The lady seated at the centre (thirteenth from left) may be Mrs Chamberlain who lived at Lacies Court and became Lady Radcliffe. It was often the practise for town tobacconists to sponsor such parties, offering ready-filled clay pipes of varied tobaccos for the clientele to sample, with a view to purchase. This may be such a party, showing one or two ladies holding their clay pipes. It also appears to be a gathering that reached, to an extent, across class divides. The residence, restored by Harry Redfern (see pages 27 and 31), now serves as the headmaster's house for Abingdon School.

St John's Road, *c.* 1930. These people are gathered in E.H. Beesley's garden after the marriage between his daughter Madge, and Aldwyn Hammond that had taken place at St Michael's church, Park Road. Standing from left: Ivy Hammond (*née* Barrett), Edward Harold Hammond (1898-1980), -?-, Wilfred Hammond (1899-1984), Madge Beesley, Aldwyn Hammond, Gladys Barrett, Oswald Barrett (1896-1983), Phyllis Beesley. Seated: -?- , Edward Alfred Hammond (1872-1944), Alice Anne Hammond (*née* Steventon) 1873-1955, Eliza Beesley, E.H.Beesley, Alice Barrett (*née* Broad) 1863-1959.

St Helen's churchyard, 1961. The Bishop of Reading (Rt Revd Eric Knell) came to Abingdon by river on a visit as Archdeacon of Berkshire and had been received at St Helen's Wharf. The bishop is being conducted to St Helen's church by the vicar of Abingdon, the Revd John H.S. Dixon and his churchwardens.

Hanney, 1945. Victory dinner served in the 1920s ex-YMCA Victory Hut which served as a village hall. Seated, second from left: Vice-Admiral William Bowden- Smith, CB, right: the Revd G.T. Shetliffe (vicar 1934-38). Standing, left: the Revd Francis Wheeler (vicar 1938-1944) Francis Wheeler became vicar of Wheatley (1944-52). George Shetliffe, was vicar of Clifton Hampden (1938-52). He married Elizabeth Mary, daughter of the Venerable R.T.A. Money-Kyrle, Archdeacon of Hereford, in 1934. After retirement to Hereford Shetliffe became honorary curate of All Saints' church. During the First World War, Admiral Bowden-Smith commanded HMS *Russell* in the Grand Fleet and at the Dardanelles, also HMS *Carnarvon* with Atlantic convoys. He was Commodore, Hong Kong (1920-22). In retirement he lived at the Old Rectory, West Hanney.

Hanney, c. 1924. Church choir, front, from left: Cyril Barrow, Wilfred Shepherd, Frederick Daubeney, Bill Taylor, Leon Picard, Hubert Tollett, Theodore Tollett, Sidney Styles, John Johns, Cyril Cox. Second row: William Cox, Charles Cox, H. Leslie Edwardes (headmaster 1896-1928), the Revd F.H. Noon (vicar 1915-1928), Aubrey Eaton (choirmaster and organist 1902-1944), Alfred Cox, Cyril Higgs, Henry Cox. Third row: Charles Styles, Leslie Dix, William Arthurs, Albert Tombs, Cleve Higgs, Bob Breakspear, Len Clinch, William Spindloe, Frank Booker. Back row: Eric Cox, Ned Sheppard, Reginald Bunce, Eric Fisher (see page 47).

East Hanney, *c.* 1906. Bearded James Robins Holmes (1859-1938) is seated on the ground next to his two sons, John and Frederick (see pages 52-54) after a tennis party at the Mulberries. J.R. Holmes described himself as bookseller and fruit grower: in reality he had a postal business in early birth control manuals and 'hygienic requisites'. He was free thinking, vegetarian and aetheist and in the hallway of his home had posted a notice in seven languages saying 'no smoking'.

West Hanney, *c.* 1946. Alice Barrett (1863-1959), wife of J.P. Barrett, the builder, as county commissioner of the Girl Guides, presents colours to the Hanney Guides at Westholme. From left: Maisie Tarry, Ruth Hubbard, Margaret Smith, Alice Barrett, Mary Lamble. The barn behind the presentation has since been converted to residential occupancy as Idian Barn.

East Hanney, c. 1900. Edgar Dandridge (1858-1922) was in partnership with his brother Alfred W. Dandridge, as miller, malster, hay, straw and corn merchant at Dandridges' Mill on the Letcombe Brook in East Hanney. By 1910, Alfred Dandridge was living at the mill house, and Edgar, known as 'King' Dandridge, at Robey Villa.

West Hanney, c. 1939. Bob Breakspear (1900-93) hauls a hayrake at Rectory Farm with Alice Maud Breakspear (1900-95). From an established village family, Bob Breakspear worked for the village builder J.P. Barrett. His wife fell out with a new vicar and she joined a particular worshipping group who still meet in the village and hold annual conventions, known to villagers as the 'Nazarines'.

Abingdon, *c.* 1972. The last Sergeant-at-Mace, Borough of Abingdon, A.K. Edwards in full dress holding the silver-gilt great mace of 1660. Virtually identical to the House of Commons mace, the Abingdon Town Clerk took it to Westminster in 1920 to compare side by side with maces from the Lords and Commons. The exercise was repeated in more recent years: Abingdon's mace reportedly being in much better condition than its Westminster counterpart.

Abingdon, *c.* 1955. Commanding officer and cadets of 2121 squadron, Air Training Corps at RAF Abingdon with a newly won trophy.

Summer Camp, July 1957. Army section, Abingdon School CCF, at Topsham Barracks, Exeter. Second row, seated, from left: David Morris (now a judge), Philip Candy, John Spinks, Ian Glenny, Brian Stacey, Nigel Hammond, CSM Wiblin (late Royal Berkshire Regt.), Capt Keith Holloway (late Royal Marines), Lt-Col Stewart Parker (late Royal Berkshire Regt.), Lt Hugh Sawbridge (late Durham Light Infantry), John Robins, George Nichol, John Mobbs, Brian Winkett, Robin Dickenson, Humphrey Bowen, John Blythe. Many of the cadets came from Abingdon and neighbouring villages.

An evacuee, 1943. Peter Crook (born 1936) was evacuated privately from Lewisham and lived with his mother, Marie Crook, in a vacant wooden hut next the Lamb inn, West Hanney. The Lamb burned down in the 1930s (see page 108), and the hut served as a beer retail outlet to retain the license until rebuilding was complete. Peter's father, George Frederick Crook, continued working in aircraft production in south east London. A bumper runner bean and tomato crop evidences 'Dig for Victory'. Country life exhilarated Peter, he eschewed an urban life and became a market gardener in Thanet, Kent.

Hanney United Football, 1946-47, players and officials. Back row, from left: Henry Broughton, Theodore Tollitt, George Cox, Arthur Watkins, Alec Belcher, Lord Ebury, Leonard Barrett, Douglas Eady, Dr Cyril Bailey, Ernie Norris, Cyril Higgs, Roy Barrett, John Broughton. Centre row: Henry Tollitt, Wilfred Barrow, Harry Nobes, David Taylor, Bob Nobes, Frank Cottrell, Wilfred Shepherd, ? Belcher. Front row: Fred Harris, Harry Shorter, Douglas Nobes, Bernard Nobes, and Percy Belcher. The team had won the North Berkshire challenge cup.

West Hanney, c. 1937. From left: Doris Mattinsley, Elizabeth Lamble, Michael Lamble, Alice Breakspear. The son of Doris Mattinsley, Brian, was evacuated privately to the village from London for the duration of the war. He lived with Alice and Bob Breakspear.

Outing to Goodwood, 1958. From left: F. Carr, J. Bunce, V. Rhodes, P. Belcher (standing), R. Bunce, Michael Lamble, M. Brennan, J. Wilkinson, R. Watkins, G. Alder, B. Nobes, Arthur Booker, Artie Wilkinson, B. Kerman, E. Norris, Alf Booker, E. Mayo, R. Broughton, Frank Cottrell (in cap), Stan Dore, Sherlin, A. Jeffries, Eric Shepherd, A. Kerman, R. Fairbrother, Jack Hayes, Arthur Watkins (walking with mackintosh), on the occasion of West Hanney's Plough Inn annual outing.

Lt-Col, the Hon Harold Greenwood Henderson, CVO, MP (1875-1922). Henderson sat as MP for North Berkshire (which constituency included and centred on Abingdon) from January 1910 to December 1918. He was the eldest son of 1st Lord Faringdon. During the South African War he served in the Lifeguards and in the First World War commanded 1/1st Berkshire Yeomanry from September 1914 until October 1915.

Declaration of Poll, February 1974. Airey Neave returned as MP for Abingdon; Neave was later assassinated immediately prior to the 1979 General Election. On his right stands Diana Neave (later Baroness Airey of Abingdon). The Conservative agent, Leslie Brown, is partly hidden behind her right arm.

The last shepherd, West Hanney, c. 1945. Jack Adams was employed by Harry Dormer at Aldworth's Farm. He and Maud Adams came from Ashbury at the foot of the Berkshire Downs, a prime sheep rearing area. They are pictured outside Shepherd's Cottage in Church Street.

Maud Adams with her husband's sheepdog, c. 1945. The story is told that normally Jack Adams did not work on Sundays so he and the dog had a well-earned day of rest. Exceptionally, one Sunday, there was a job to do out in the fields, but the highly intelligent sheepdog, upon hearing the distant Hanney church bells, dashed off from the sheepfold to take refuge at home and maintain its required day of rest at Shepherd's Cottage.

Abingdon, 1914. Starting their journey to the trenches, Abingdon men march along Ock Street. Some 1,400 Abingdonians fought in the First World War and 228 names are recorded on the town's war memorial unveiled in 1921 by the 7th Earl of Abingdon, High Steward of the Borough.

Harwell, c. 1910. Richard Rice (left) winning a hundred yard sprint while a medical student at the London Hospital. He won two silver cups in the hundred metres at the International Olympic Grand Prix at Ghent. Rice was member of Surrey AC and Reading AC and founded Harwell Football Club in 1911 becoming a playing member.

Harwell, c. 1910. Richard Goodenough Rice (1886-1939), sprinter, hurdler and Olympic athlete. Rice competed in the 1912 Stockholm Olympic Games and in the Antwerp Olympics. He was one of four sons of Dr Richard Rice (1859-1947), veteran Harwell doctor and during the First World War was in the Royal Garrison Artillery seeing service in France. Young Richard was at Abingdon School from 1895-1903, with two of his brothers, where he was known as a superb all-round athlete and sportsman. He was a keen bellringer and a well-known member of the North Berks branch of the Oxford Diocesan Guild of Church Bellringers. In later years he wrote regular football reports for *The North Berks Herald*.

Abingdon, 1874. The Ven Alfred Pott, BD (1822-1908), vicar of Abingdon (1868-75) and Archdeacon of Berkshire (1870-1903). Pott had previously been vicar of Cuddesdon and Principal of Cuddesdon Theological College as a protégé of Bishop Wilberforce of Oxford. He was rector of East Hendred (1857-59), vicar of Clifton Hampden (1875-82) and vicar of Sonning (1882-99). He notes in a personal autobiography that the Revd W.J. Butler, vicar of Wantage, commented to him prior to his preferment to Abingdon that 'anyone taking Abingdon must expect to be burned in the market place before much can be done.' Nevertheless, while at Abingdon he oversaw the restoration of St Helen's church and the building of a new National School. This oil portrait by Rodney was painted on Pott's resignation from Abingdon. In 1928 G. Stanley Pott gave it to Abingdon School.

Lyford almshouses, c.1900. These almshouses were founded by Oliver Ayshcombe in 1711. The Revd Frederick Hill Currie (1832-1925), perpetual curate of Lyford (1897-1924), for a £40 salary read prayers each morning as chaplain. Currie resigned from Lyford in 1924 being then over ninety years old. A letter from Currie in the Bodleian Library, responding as an old boy to Abingdon School Boat Club appeal (1901) says: 'the smallness of the stipend received from this perpetual curacy hinders my helping in this and like matters.'

West Hanney, c. 1865. The Revd James Macdougall (1812-1896) was curate of Hanney 1846-49 and vicar 1849-92, consequently being associated with the village for almost fifty years. In the Victorian period a ministry of such length for a country parson was not an unusual circumstance. His paternalism and benevolence included a temperance reading room and laundry where, for the villagers, a warm bath might also be had. He acted as parish waywarden (1880) and left funds to Lyford almshouses for the use of West Hanney elderly, to be known as Macdougall's Almshouse, and he purchased in- and out-patient recommendations at Oxford's Radcliffe Infirmary for sick villagers. Perhaps inspired by life in East and West Hanney at that time, he wrote a tract called 'Sleeping in Church'.

Abingdon, 1974. Eric Anderson (headmaster Abingdon School 1970-75), with Mrs Margaret Thatcher MP, Dennis Thatcher, Sir George Sinclair MP (chairman of governors and member for Dorking) and Airey Neave MP. Mrs Thatcher had inaugurated building works for a new dining hall in Park Crescent.

Eight
Work and Play

East Hanney, *c.* 1920. Hanney school morris dancers, started by headmaster H. Leslie Edwardes (1863-1936) and Mrs Edwardes. Press reports indicate the troupe was much in demand and well received, travelling to Abingdon, Wantage and intermediate villages to demonstrate their talents.

Abingdon, c. 1955. St Helen's water mill as a working enterprise, standing over the River Ock close to is confluence with the Thames. This substantial mill, with the original building of the National School attached on the eastern side, is wedged between the two rivers, Christ's Hospital and St Helen's churchyard. The mill is now in residential occupancy.

Abingdon, 1960. Housewives busy shopping at a Monday pre-Christmas market day.

Grove, c. 1920. Hanney Magpies concert party with their village audience were photographed by A.W. Booker, the village photographer, following a performance in Grove National School.

Abingdon, c. 1965. Play time in the river slipway at the foot of East St Helen Street where the Borough Ford may have crossed the river to Andersey Island. Replaced by Abingdon Bridge in 1416, the bridge is still known as Burford Bridge as a corruption of Borough Ford Bridge.

Near Abingdon, *c.* 1880. Evocative haymaking scene in a riverside meadow in May or early June. Three workmen are about to lead a fully laden wagon hauled by a pair of horses off to a rickyard. Walkers converse on the bridge beyond escaped sheep on the towing path.

Abingdon, *c.* 1955. Town centre view, looking towards the market place and East St Helen Street. Much of the area around the cattle market was cleared in the 1960s for Bury Street shopping precinct. Stratton Way does not exist, Ock Street sand Bath Street consequently remain intact. Viewed from aloft it is easy to see what upheaval the 1960s brought to the town.

Steventon, August 1891. In December 1956 Mrs H.M. Gerring of the Causeway wrote to *Berkshire Life*, saying: 'my husband is of an old village family of carpenters. My son, now twenty-five, is the sixth generation in Steventon to carry on business. The photograph outside our present old workshop…shows my son's great-grandfather and his two brothers and family. The old timber wagon can clearly be seen on the left.'

Garford, *c.* 1965. Frederick and Ida Ayris with young Elsa Ayris outside part of his blacksmith's workshop on the western side of the village opposite the former College Farm. Over several generations the family had operated Hinton Waldrist and Garford forge, Marcham brick kiln and a haulage business at Gozzard's Ford.

Abingdon, c. 1810. Michaelmas fair in High Street. At the centre a recruiting sergeant attempts to engage some country lads to take the King's shilling. On the left a farmer notes an arrangement to hire a man. Women seek work as domestic servants. The lad in the background holding a whip aloft with a ribbon tied around it is seeking work as a carter.

Abingdon, c. 1950. Michaelmas fair extended through the town from market place to the far end of Ock Street. It was successor to the hiring fair where men seeking work as ploughmen, fodderers, shepherds, cowmen or general farm labourers came to seek a new employer. Some, unhappy with their posting, came back the following week to seek alternative work at the 'runaway fair'.

West Hendred, c. 1906. Three girls at play outside cottages at Ginge Road and Church Lane. This is Eleanor Hayden's village, where she was the vicar's daughter and author of *Travels Round our Village* (1901), which she may have had in mind when she wrote: 'it is good in these days of bustle and strife, to drift for a while into some quiet backwater...which the tide of progress stirs but just enough to avert stagnation; where old world customs and archaic forms of speech still linger and where men go about their daily tasks in a spirit of serene leisureliness.'

East Hendred, c. 1955. This timber framed village shop built in splendid early Tudor domestic style may previously have been home to one of the wealthy village wool merchants.

Abingdon, *c.* 1920. John George Timothy West (1860-1931), architect, who had been articled to Edwin Dolby. Timothy West was responsible for numerous buildings in Abingdon including the chapel and 1901 extension at Abingdon School and houses is the area of Albert Park. Timothy West was succeeded in the architectural profession by his son, Archibald Buller West (1885-1957) and grandson, Duncan Buller West (see page 37).

West Hanney, *c.* 1900. The Lamb Inn, burnt down and rebuilt in the 1930s. The publican's house is on the left with entry to the bar in the centre. Entry to the windowless cattle shed on the right may also have accessed the feed and hayloft above. Barns and sheds surround, denoting a time when the publican was part farmer and part innkeeper. Parish records stored at the inn were destroyed in the blaze.

Nine

Abingdon and the Villages

Abingdon, 1939. Two almswomen in conversation in the garden of Christ's Hospital. This is one of a series of photographs published in *The Times* and contained in an album presented by the newspaper to the archives of Christ's Hospital. (Copyright: *The Times*)

Abingdon, 1875. This is the Albert Park area of the town. Park and Conduit Roads are largely undeveloped and Park Crescent housing is only partly built. This is a map of Abingdon before Exbourne Road, Bostock Road and St Michael's Avenue exist.

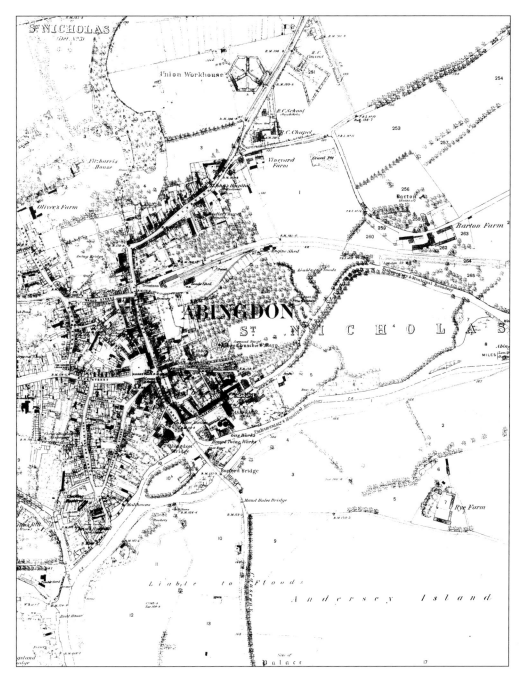

Abingdon, 1875. Around the town centre commerce and manufacturing jostle for space with housing requirements.

Abingdon, 1960. Twickenham House, East St Helen Street, built for Joseph Tomkins, around 1756. The cupola, invisible from the street, joins several others in the town notably at county hall, the hall of Christ's Hospital, Mr Twitty's almshouses and the clockhouse in Ock Street.

Lower Radley, 1960. A timber-framed cottage having an agricultural provenance, built in local vernacular style with red brick and thatch.

Radley College, *c.* 1909. A Warland Andrew photograph of the north entrance to the school. Buildings are from left: A Social, Croome's Tower and F Social, formerly Long Dorm.

Radley College, *c.* 1909. The Hall, formerly the Warden's House, was built in 1721-27 by William Townsend and was originally the home of Sir George Bowyer who had been fraudulently persuaded that extensive coal seams existed under the estate. The Hall was then let to a non-conformist school but when the lease returned to the market, the Revd Dr William Sewell of Exeter College, Oxford, took the house, opening it as St Peter's College, Radley, on 9 June 1847.

West Hanney, *c.* 1900. Looking north from the village green along Winter Lane, so named by association with the cold northerly direction of its course. The only house extant is Castleacre (right). Modern development now extends each side of the road in former orchards and over the site of Rectory Farm.

West Hanney, *c.* 1900. Main Street looking east. All but three of the buildings have been demolished and this part of the village has been redeveloped during the last half century. The Hanneys, like many surrounding settlements, were heavily reliant on agriculture and consequently supported an economically poor population. The Royal Commission on Labour, 1893, published *The Agricultural Labourer* as its report. The commission held public enquiries specifically into conditions at East and West Hanney and reported that most people were living in unsatisfactory, overcrowded housing, inadequately ventilated, without satisfactory sanitation, water supply or heating. Built often only partly of brick, with wattle, thatch, low ceilings and unmade earth floors, the cottages were natural candidates for redevelopment in the 1920s and after.

West Hanney, c. 1930. Declared unsafe around 1927, the upper stage of the church tower was demolished in 1940 and rebuilt in 1960, having during the Second World War a 'bonnet' of second-hand corrugated iron which became an eye-sore, but covered the remaining stages and kept out the weather. The present roof is designed so that at some future date it may have a spire added.

Buckland, 1890. Henry Taunt posed this conversation piece in Summerside, then an unmade road at the south of the village.

Buckland, 1912. North terrace of Buckland House. The central section was built by J. Wood the younger of Bath in 1757 for Sir Robert Throckmorton. Projecting wings in matching style were added in 1910 by Romaine Walker.

Buckland, 1920. A late seventeenth-century manor house, it was converted in the late eighteenth century to gothic-style stables for Buckland House. What appears as a clock above the central doorway does in fact record the direction of the wind – a useful item for huntsmen leaving the stables.

Kingston Bagpuize, 1960. St John the Baptist's church (1799-1800) was built by John Fidel of Faringdon, but had an apse added and was internally altered in 1882 by Edwin Dolby of Abingdon.

Pusey House, 1960. This was built in 1753 to the design of J. Wood of Bath. Of the Pusey family, Philip Pusey was an agricultural innovator, and the Revd Edward Bouverie-Pusey (1800-82) a prominent leader of the Oxford Movement, after whom Pusey House in St Giles' is named.

Appleton, 1960. The late Norman church of St Lawrence holds a handsome Elizabethan tomb to Sir John Fettiplace (1593). The church is next to the ancient manor house, one of several homes of the Fettiplace family and held here until 1600. The Fettiplaces were resident at North Denchworth in 1263 but Childrey was their principal seat (1263-1806). They once held thirty-one manors and land in fifteen counties. The family name became extinct in 1743 but by Act of Parliament a descendant assumed the name. However, that line also came to an end in 1806. They possessed property locally at West Shefford, Denchworth, Besselsleigh and Swinbrook near Burford. At Swinbrook there are uniquely arranged tombs to six Fettiplaces stacked one above the other each side of the chancel.

Fyfield, 1960. The road from Fyfield Wick into the village centre, seen before the Fyfield and Kingston Bagpuize bypass cut this southern part of the village from its core.

Besselsleigh, 1960. Gatepier of the demolished Besselsleigh manor, in mid-seventeenth century style and notably similar to gatepiers at Sutton Courtenay manor. In 1350 Besselsleigh was owned by the Bessels family from Provence. Sir Peter Bessels (died 1424) gave stone for the 1416 bridges at Abingdon and Culham, also leaving money for their upkeep. There is a portrait of Sir Peter Bessils presented in 1607 and hanging in the Hall of Christ's Hospital, Abingdon.

Charney Bassett, *c.* 1910. West front of the manor house. Eleanor Hayden in *Islands of the Vale* records how one tenant of the manor 'was in the habit of bestowing sixpence at Christmas on every child in the place. His discrimination, however, did not keep pace with his benevolence, and naughty boys and girls after having received their coins would scamper home, change their raiment, disfigure their faces, and thus disguised would join the tail of the procession and boldly present themselves for a second gift. The Vale people are a simple folk!'

South Hinksey, 1960. The solidly built and unbuttressed west tower of St Lawrence's church. The village is reached by a footpath from Oxford called Jacob's Ladder or Elephant Back. It was the walking ground of Matthew Arnold who turned once to watch 'the line of festal lights in Christ Church Hall'. The Hinkseys were the gateway for Arnold's walks into the 'warm green-muffled Cumnor Hills' by way of the 'Happy Valley' passing Childsworth Farm and Signal Elm to Cumnor Hurst and Boar's Hill, and referred to at length in 'Thyrsis and Scholar Gipsy.' 'In the Hinkseys nothing keeps the same.'

Long Wittenham, 1960. One of the most delightful and oldest Thameside inns, the Barley Mow. Originally of cruck constuction, built about 1350, the inn has in recent years been partly destroyed by fire but rebuilt with modern additions. Jerome K. Jerome's *Three Men in a Boat* tied up at this 'fairy-tale inn'.

Clifton Hampden, 1955. Old thatch, village shop, church and Clifton Bridge. The bridge was designed by Sir George Gilbert Scott and built with finely made brick from the estate brickyard. The church was also restored by Scott.

Appleford, 1960. An early spring walk for two village ladies under stately elms. The largely Victorian church of St Peter and St Paul has buried in its churchyard reputedly the world's oldest jockey, John Faulkner (1829-1933). As a youngster of eight he rode his first winner: at the other end of his career in 1903 he rode his last race at Abingdon at the age of 74. He lived another thirty years and died in 1933 on the eve of his 105th birthday.

Steventon, 1960. One of I.K. Brunel's houses in the station yard built around 1840. The buildings were used for board meetings of the GWR from 1842-43 when Steventon, conveniently halfway between Paddington and Bristol, was used as the company headquarters until transferred to London. Another house acted as hotel for passengers travelling to and from Oxford and Abingdon. From 1840 to 1844 eight road coaches a day made the journey to Oxford, but in June 1844 the line from Didcot to Oxford was opened and Steventon lost its prominent position on the railway.

Garford, 1960. Millett's Farmhouse was built in Lockinge Estate style as are other buildings in the village. The roof shows an elegant pattern of tiles.

Milton, 1960. The Manor House was built in 1630 to the design of Inigo Jones. The spacious library, completed 1771, is decorated in Strawberry Hill Gothic, a style in vogue for twenty years from 1760.

Sutton Courtenay, 1960. The Norman Hall is of late twelfth-century origin. Around 1640 some farsighted owner turned the Hall into a farmhouse, but originally it may have been a chapel, for which purpose it is correctly oriented.

Drayton, c. 1900. The unmade High Street leads east. On the left Walnut Cottage faces the entry to Cheer's Farm. The barn beyond is part of Drayton Manor, with opposite a notable cruck-constructed cottage.

Milton Hill, c. 1910. Kate Carvey is sitting in the front row (second from left), the daughter of James Carvey (1855-1928) horse clipper of Wantage. She worked for Sir Mortimer Singer (1863-1929) at Milton Hill House. Singer, born Yonkers, New York, developed the sewing machine and moved to Britain in 1900 taking citizenship. A pioneer in cycling, motoring and flying, he was a breeder, trainer and exhibitor of horses (hunters, jumpers and harness horses). Giving his house over for a military hospital during the First World War, he moved to Steventon House nearby. For this and other philanthropic work he was awarded a KBE in 1920 (see page 52).

Acknowledgements

I am grateful to those people who offered photographs, many from unpublished family collections of Abingdon and the surrounding villages, also to those who suggested interpretations for the more mysterious images. This book has been made possible by the help and generosity of the following:

Abingdon School Archives (Mrs Sarah Wearne),

The Master and Governers of Christ's Hospital, Abingdon, (Mr David Barrett, Master),

Mrs Joyce Parsons (Abingdon), Mr Basil Ayris (Abingdon),The late Mr Ron Chung,

Mr Alan Steeves-Booker (Shorncote), Mrs Yvonne Drakes (Cabourne),

Drayton Local History Group, Hanney History Group, Mr and Mrs N.W. Stimpson (Drayton)

Mrs Ann Townsend (Grove), Mrs Valerie Reason (East Hanney),

Mr Peter Crook (Thanet), Mr Brian Mattinsley (Milton Keynes),

Mr Edward Lay (Harwell), Mrs Sally Saxby (Lymington),

Mrs Jacqueline Smith (Abingdon), *The Abingdonian, The North Berkshire Herald,*

The Times, Mr Nigel Eady (West Hanney), Miss Rosemary Pryor (Didcot),

Mr Robin Pryor (Didcot), Mr David Barrett (Abingdon),

Mr Charles Parker (Buckland), Mr Hugh Randolph (Abingdon),

Mr David Flint (Garford), Mr Henry Midwinter (Steventon),

Mrs Doris Barrow (West Hanney), Mrs V. Vickers (East Hanney),

Oxfordshire Library Service (Abingdon and Wantage Local History Collections), the Bodleian Library and Pusey House Library, Oxford, also numerous people who have been helpful in assembling this book.

Bibliography

Books and Publications consulted:

Travels around our Village (1901) and *Islands of the Vale,*Eleanor Hayden (1908); *A History of Abingdon* (1910, reprinted 1970) and *News of a Country Town* (1914), James Townsend; *St Nicholas and Other Papers* (1929, reprinted 1971) and *Christ's Hospital, Abingdon* (1929), Arthur E. Preston; *Inns and Alehouses of Abingdon 1550-1978,* Jacqueline Smith and John Carter (1978); *Abingdon in Camera,* M.J. Thomas (1979); *A History of Rowing at Abingdon School, 1840-1990,* R.G. Mortimer (1990); *Holmes of Hanney,* Frank Poller (1993); *The Berkshire Yeomanry,* A. Verey, S. Sampson, A. French, S. Frost (1994); *Around Abingdon,* Nigel Hammond (1996); *The Martlet and the Griffen,* Thomas Hinde and Michael St J. Parker (1997).